Nova Scotia

Nova Scotia

Whitecap Books

North Vancouver • British Columbia • Canada

Canadian Cataloguing in publication Data

Main entry under title:

Nova Scotia

ISBN 0-920620-65-5

1. Nova Scotia — Description and travel —
1950   — Views.* I. Jones, J. E. (Jeanette Elaine),
1945-
FC2312.N68 1985   917.16'0022'2   C85-091128-1
F1037.8.N68   1985

Designed by Michael E. Burch
Printed by D. W. Friesen & Sons Ltd.
Altona, Manitoba

© **Whitecap Books Ltd.**
1086 W. 3rd Street
North Vancouver, B.C., Canada

First Edition 1985

Printed in Canada

Nova Scotia — A Brief History

Fog-shrouded headlands, sun-drenched sandy beaches, picturesque lighthouses and a breathtaking trail around one of the world's most undeniably beautiful islands are just some of the images that reflect the Province of Nova Scotia.

But the province is more than just pretty pictures. Nova Scotia was in the vanguard of European settlement of North America. It saw the very beginnings of Canada, grew through the dreadful privations of those first winters of settlement, survived the contest of France and England for control of the territories, mourned the misfortunes of the Acadians, and was present at the birth of Canada, as one of the founding colonies. A pride in this history with its many cultural strands, the pervasive influence of the sea and a proud maritime tradition, and a large measure of natural beauty combine to form the Nova Scotia of today.

Nova Scotia's first people were the Micmacs. Tall and athletic, they hunted in the forests and harvested the sea. They also made use of the natural bounty of the land: roots, berries, plants and the sap of the maple tree, boiled down to make cakes. They had many festivals, including the Feast of St. Aspinquid, celebrated annually on the shores of what is now North West Arm in Halifax. This festival was in honour of the chief of all the northern tribes, and was shared with the European newcomers after the establishment of a British colony at Halifax. But, like other native people of North America, the Micmacs were easy prey for imported European diseases, and their numbers were drastically depleted. Originally estimated at 25,000, their population in Nova Scotia now numbers approximately 6000. Little is known of the remote ancestors of Nova Scotia's Micmac Indians, but remains have been found of a people dating back about 11000 years; they were caribou hunters who used stone tools and who may have entered North America via a polar land bridge.

The first European visitors to Nova Scotia were probably Norse. Long before the search for a Northwest Passage and a penchant for furs brought European interest, fishermen had been trekking across the North Atlantic to the Grand Banks off Newfoundland for the plentiful cod supply. It is thought that some of the Norse fishermen landed on these shores approximately 1000 years ago.

In 1497 John Cabot planted the flag of England on Cape Breton soil, but it was to be over a century before any serious attempt was made to settle these new lands.

By the 17th Century, France was becoming interested in establishing a French presence in North America to compete with British and Spanish exploration. Furs and fish were abundant in the north, and England and Spain were already established further to the south, so France cast her eye north. In 1599 an expedition led by Chauvin and Pont-Gravé (who had been granted a generous monopoly in the territory) left 16 men at Tadoussac. Unprepared for the harsh winter, this expedition was a failure, but it did interest one influential passenger, Pierre de Gua, Sieur de Monts, in the new land. As a result, he formed a company, was commissioned Vice Admiral and Lieutenant-General of New France, and was granted a 10 year fur trade monopoly and customs exemption on all goods imported from France. Their 1604 expedition met with one of the coldest winters in history, and in the spring the survivors left their base at Ile Saint Croix to find a more hospitable site. After searching the coastline to Cape Cod, they settled on Port Royal, and in the summer of 1605, the first permanent settlement in Canada was established there.

The next year saw the added refinement of a water-driven grist mill — the previous summer had proved the fertility of the soil with abundant crops — and perhaps more important, the establishment, by Poutrincourt and

Champlain, of what was indubitably the first social club in North America: the Order of Good Cheer. With another winter under their belts, cultivation underway, and the camaraderie of their fellows, these early settlers triumphed over enormous odds. They were fortunate, too, in having the friendship of Chief Membertou, who was a great ally. Relations between native Indians and the French were good at Port Royal, and many feasts were shared.

But the promise of the settlement was not immediately realized; the following year the fur monopoly was revoked and Port Royal was abandoned. Determined to return to Port Royal, Poutrincourt took samples of the remarkable abundance of the land — rye, corn, flax and other crops — to show to the French court. He did return in 1610, but three years later, during his absence, the fort was sacked and burned by a privateer employed by British colonists at Jamestown. The few remaining colonists wintered with the Indians and Poutrincourt returned to France, his dreams shattered.

Meanwhile, England had not forgotten her new possession (Cabot had claimed all of North America for England when he landed on Cape Breton) but colonizing efforts had met with little success. In 1621 King James I of Scotland granted the area now known as Nova Scotia to Sir William Alexander, creating the Order of Baronets of Nova Scotia to encourage settlement there. Any Scot who financed a certain number of settlers to Nova Scotia could receive a Baronetcy and title to 30,000 acres of land in Nova Scotia. Settlement was still slow.

When war broke out between France and England in 1627, Alexander set out with his fleet to destroy French possessions in North America. He managed to take Port Royal and establish his own colony here, but the treaty of 1629 decreed the return of all possessions taken within two years of its signing. Port Royal was returned to the French. Although his colonizing efforts failed, Sir William Alexander left his legacy to Nova Scotia: the name of the province, and the coat of arms, granted by King Charles I in 1625, which was to become the basis for the flag of Nova Scotia.

In 1632, forty French families were settled in the area surrounding Port Royal, and during the next two decades the French presence was firmly established in the land known as Acadia. These settlers were farmers who had a deep love for the land and a preference for a simple pastoral lifestyle. They settled in the rich river valleys, making the soil even more productive by diking, and becoming almost entirely dependent on the land and each other, far from the battles and skirmishes of European Imperialism. They had a productive relationship with the native Indians, and from them they learned the uses of native plants and berries, how to hunt wild game and tap the sweet sap of the maple tree.

But in Europe pressures were building. While the French fought amongst themselves for control of the lucrative fur trade, England was strengthening the navy which would give her dominance over a far-flung empire. In 1652 Port Royal and Fort LaTour were taken by the English navy, with the aid of New Englanders, and although the Treaty of Westminster in 1655 noted that Acadia was still French, it remained English, and the area continued to be a battleground for the next 50 years, with French, English, New Englanders and Indians combining to produce a constantly changing balance of power.

In 1710, British forces captured Port Royal for the final time. The Treaty of Utrecht, in 1713, ended the history of Acadia as a French colony. By the terms of the treaty, Acadia (or Nova Scotia) was granted to the British and Isle Royale (Cape Breton) to the French. In short order, the strategic significance of Isle Royale was realized, and work was begun on Fortress Louisbourg, one of the most ambitious fortifications to be constructed in North America.

By 1742 the garrisons stationed at Fortress Louisbourg numbered up to 1700 and a complex society had evolved within the walls of the fort. Taverns and small shops supported the life of the town and the narrow streets contained an array of homes suitable to the powerful rulers of the colony and the artisans who supplied the needs of the townspeople. Outside the walls, the colony was growing as well, and by 1738 the total population of the colony was 4,000, and many small fishing villages had taken root along the coast.

When the Treaty of Utrecht granted Port Royal to the British, the Acadians living in the area were given two years to either swear an oath of allegiance to Britain or to dispose of their property and leave. They were encouraged to relocate at Isle Royale, where land was offered, but for a variety of reasons many Acadians chose not to go. The following decade saw a series of attempts by the British to bring about their acquiescence, but it would be another 30 years before the final chapter would be written in the sad story of the Acadians in Nova Scotia.

In 1744 France and England were again at war, and this time they looked to their outposts in North America. Annapolis (Port Royal was renamed Annapolis Royal by the British in honour of Queen Anne) was the English bastion in Nova Scotia, while Louisbourg guarded the entrance of New France. Louisbourg fell, was restored to France in 1747 by the Treaty of Aix-La-Chapelle, but within a decade it fell to England for the last time. The Siege of Louisbourg, 1758, lasted 48 days. The clever and courageous General Wolfe went on to win the Battle of the Plains of Abraham at Quebec the following year, marking an end to French domination of colonization in North America. By 1760 Fortress Louisbourg, the proud symbol of French colonialism, was demolished.

The British needed further protection of their interests in Nova Scotia, and in 1749 Halifax was established. The first settlers responded to ads in a London paper offering free transport, tools, a year's rations and 50 acres of land plus 10 acres for each family member. From the beginning the little settlement put down firm, deep roots, and by the following summer they had a hospital, a school and plans for St. Paul's Church, Canada's first Anglican Church. Steadfastly British, Halifax was the military, cultural and government centre for the British in North America. The following year, Dartmouth was founded by a further 353 settlers.

To counterbalance the Acadians, some 2700 Protestant Europeans were imported; some of these settled in Halifax and some went on to found Lunenburg. Of stalwart farming stock, these settlers were to turn to the sea and become world renowned for their prowess in fishing and boatbuilding.

By 1755 the struggle for control of the colonies in North America had intensified and it was no longer possible to ignore the position of the Acadians in British territory. A peaceful people, probably with little understanding of the events which were shaping their lives, they were nevertheless a threat to British security. Evidence was produced which indicated that some Acadians, in conjunction with Indian allies, were not merely a passive threat but were actively involved in French-English struggles. On the other hand, Acadians who were willing to take a British oath of allegiance demanded protection; they were afraid of the Indians turning against them if they did take the oath, as the Indians had consistently allied themselves with the French and specifically with the priest LeLoutre.

French-English hostilities escalated, the very size of the Acadian population was threatening and the strategic importance of Halifax was threatened. While the Acadians wanted an oath which would give them neutrality, the English were unable to make any compromises. On July 28, 1755, the Council of Halifax made the decision to expel the Acadians from their lands, and transport them by sea to other colonies in North America. On September 5 the historic proclamation was read at Grand Pré by Colonel John Winslow. Captain Alexander Murray at Piziquid and Major

John Handfield at Annapolis carried out the orders of Council.

The families that were inadvertently separated, the loss of land and possessions, and the terrible uprooting of a long tradition were the price paid by the Acadians for standing in the way of forces beyond their control and understanding. The powers in faraway Europe had dictated their fate decades before, and new political forces were taking independent shape in the new world.

Within its first ten years Halifax had grown into a solid community and by 1758 the demand for an elected assembly was granted. Now New Englanders could be imported to open up the land and to populate the land vacated by the Acadians. Boatloads of settlers, attracted by advertising, came from New England, forming the basis of towns such as Truro, Onslow, Newport, Amherst, Sackville and Cumberland. Hardworking and experienced in the new world, some 4500 New Englanders made great inroads into the settlement of the wilderness, bringing with them the British parliamentary system and the independence of spirit which would ensure its application.

In the next decade the towns of Clare, Pubnico and Tusket were settled by repatriated Acadians, who now wished to take the oath. They were given 80 acres of land and assurance of freedom of worship.

Settlement of the north shore of Nova Scotia was begun around 1770. The earliest settlers were New Englanders, at Pictou. Three years later the *Hector* sailed from Scotland with 33 families and 25 bachelors aboard, the first of a substantial number of Scottish settlers who would come to this area. During this same period 11 shiploads of Yorkshiremen, numbering about 1000, came to Nova Scotia, settling in Chignecto and then dispersing throughout the territory.

During the American Revolution, the population of Nova Scotia was swelled by a further influx of New Englanders. Approximately 25,000 Loyalists — conservative, hardworking, and loyal to Britain — formed an important component of Nova Scotia, with ties to both England and the United States. After the War of 1812, several thousand Blacks settled in the Halifax-Dartmouth area; the early 1800s saw 50,000 Highland Scots settle in Cape Breton Island, Pictou and Antigonish.

By the turn of the century settlement of Nova Scotia was well on its way. Small settlements huddled together and though the roots were not yet deep they were firmly planted. The main cultural streams of Nova Scotia were present; later would come the many other nationalities which make up the cultural mix of Nova Scotia today.

In 1841 Halifax was incorporated as a city — the first elected municipal government in Nova Scotia. The following decades saw debates rage over union of the colonies. The first responsible government in the empire outside Great Britain was established here in 1848. James Uniacke was the first colonial premier, followed by William Young, J. W. Johnston, Joseph Howe — the firebrand premier who pioneered freedom of the press — and Sir Charles Tupper, active in the Union movement, one of the four Founding Fathers of Confederation, and Prime Minister of Canada in 1896.

The past century has brought growth and prosperity to Nova Scotia, but the independence of spirit and courage of conviction of those early settlers is still found in Maritimers today. The fishery which once brought explorers and settlers to Nova Scotia remains the principle industry in the province. Mining, agriculture and tourism are also important to the economy of Nova Scotia, but the great abundance of the sea and its powerful influence remains the single most important factor in the identity of the province. No part of Nova Scotia is more than 56 km (35 mi.) from the sea, and even the most urban of city-dwellers feels a part of the maritime tradition. A spectacularly indented coastline of 7,400 km (4,625 mi.) provides safe harbours for the myriad of fishing villages with their dories, fishboats of all sizes, weatherworn sheds, nets, pilings and lobster pots — all of which delight the heart of any visitor.

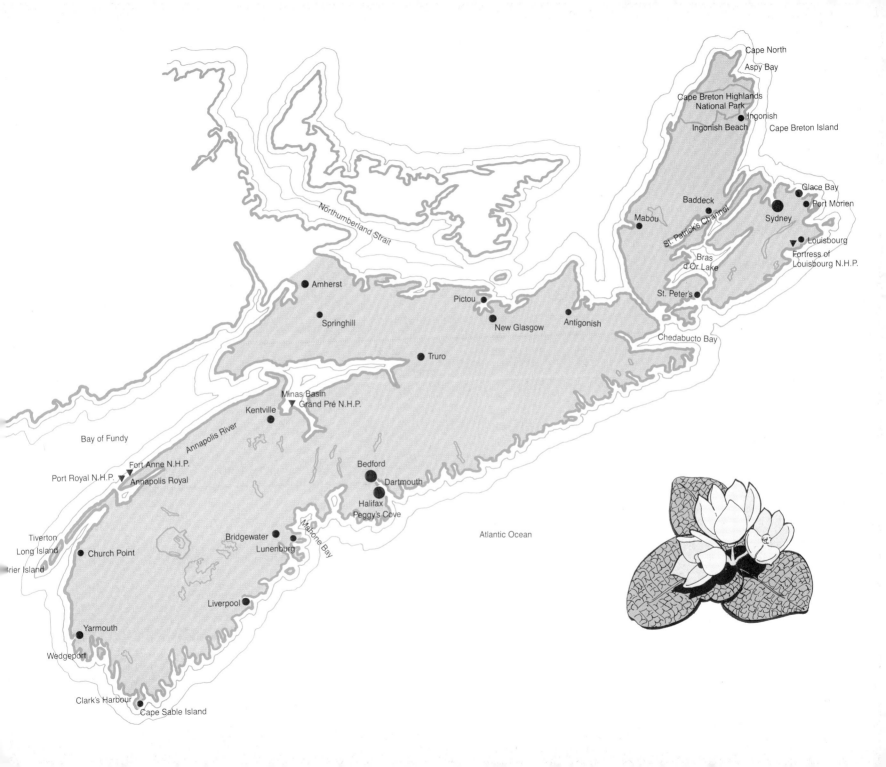

Cape North
Aspy Bay
Cape Breton Highlands National Park
Ingonish
Ingonish Beach
Cape Breton Island
Glace Bay
Baddeck
Port Morien
Mabou
St. Patrick's Channel
Sydney
Louisbourg
Fortress of Louisbourg N.H.P.
Bras d'Or Lake
St. Peter's
Chedabucto Bay
Northumberland Strait
Amherst
Pictou
Springhill
New Glasgow
Antigonish
Truro
Minas Basin
Grand Pré N.H.P.
Kentville
Bay of Fundy
Annapolis River
Fort Anne N.H.P.
Bedford
Port Royal N.H.P.
Dartmouth
Annapolis Royal
Halifax
Peggy's Cove
Tiverton
Long Island
Bridgewater
Mahone Bay
Brier Island
Church Point
Lunenburg
Atlantic Ocean
Liverpool
Yarmouth
Wedgeport
Clark's Harbour
Cape Sable Island

Halifax

Halifax was founded as a garrison town by the English in 1749. From the beginning it was both a military and a commercial centre, and the Halifax of today carries on those traditions as the capital of Nova Scotia.

The first city in British North America, Halifax quickly set down its cultural roots, becoming a city of 'firsts'. It had the first public school in Canada, the first printing press, newspaper, Protestant church, dockyard and post office. It had the first public gardens, begun in 1753. It even had the first tennis courts.

The modern structures of this progressive city provide an interesting contrast to its well-preserved old buildings (heritage is important to Haligonians). The old waterfront warehouses, once used by privateers, have been restored and converted to small, charming shops and services, and a huge urban redevelopment program in part of the harbour includes modern highrises housing business, retail services, apartments and a shopping mall.

The Old Clock Tower, erected in 1802 by the Duke of Kent, is a landmark in Halifax.

11

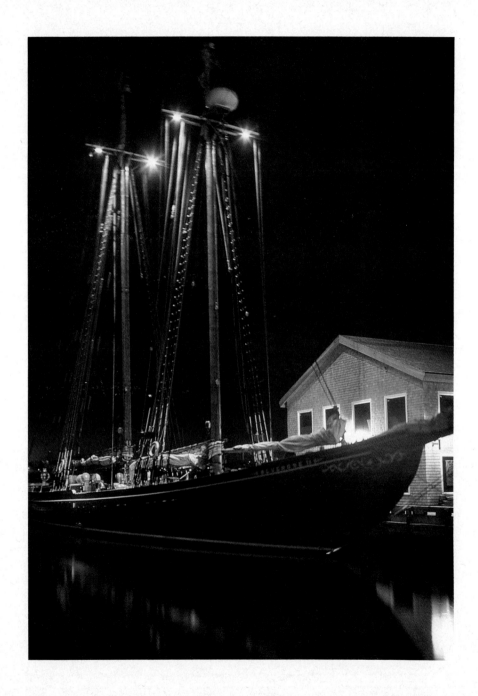

The *Bluenose*

Most famous of the Lunenburg schooners was the *Bluenose*, unequalled champion of the Atlantic fishing fleet during the 1920s and 30s. Amazingly fast, and beautifully constructed in the classic style, the *Bluenose* came from a long line of fishing schooners built for speed and strength (they sailed to the Grand Banks off Newfoundland for their catch).

The *Bluenose II*, pictured here, is a faithful copy of the original — 42.9 m. long (143 ft.) with 3,048 sq. metres (10,000 sq. ft.) of sail. It is berthed in Halifax and gives public cruises. The original *Bluenose* is commemorated on the Canadian dime.

Opposite: Huge container ships transport goods to and from Halifax harbour.

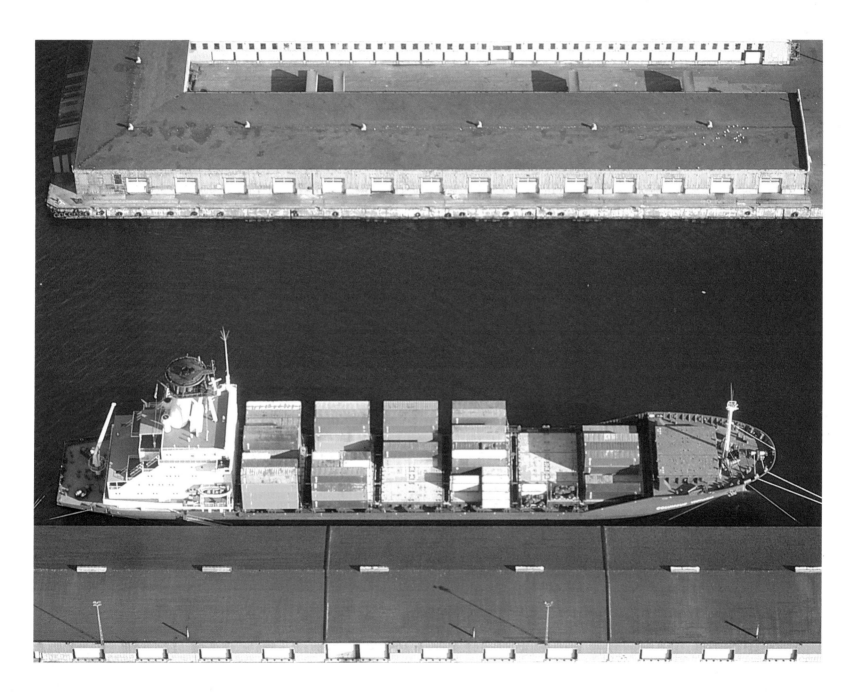

Old rowhouses on a downtown Halifax street.

The interior of St. Paul's Church, erected in 1750 and the oldest Anglican church in Canada.

The Citadel

Opposite: Halifax's distinctive star-shaped Citadel overlooks the bustling city. The hilltop fortress was constructed between 1828 and 1856, but earlier fortifications were here as early as 1749, and it was the headquarters for Prince Edward when he commanded the military here from 1794 to 1800.

Today the Citadel is open to the public and contains the Army Museum. From here there is an excellent view of Halifax, the harbour to the left and the Northwest Arm to the right, and Dartmouth across the harbour.

The Halifax Public Gardens are based on gardens started in 1753 and were formally established in 1867. Fountains, a bandstand, formal flower bed arrangements and many exotic species of plants imported from around the world, are some of the features of this fine garden.

Halifax Harbour and Dartmouth

The twin cities of Halifax and Dartmouth share one of the world's great harbours and deepest ports. Extending 16 km (10 mi.) inland, the harbour has a narrow neck which opens into the wide waters of Bedford Basin. It is constantly busy with a myriad of vessels: ocean liners, military ships, industrial shipping, fishing boats and pleasure craft.

Dartmouth, founded in 1750, remained a small rural centre until it was connected via the Angus L. MacDonald Bridge to Halifax. Dartmouth was incorporated in 1961 and now includes an industrial and residential area with a population of approximately 62,000. It is known as 'the city of lakes' for good reason — within its boundaries lie 23 lakes.

The Angus L. MacDonald Bridge, completed in 1955.

Peggy's Cove is a photographer's paradise and one of the most famous scenic areas in North America.

The buildings and byways of Peggy's Cove can be just as scenic as its famous lighthouse.

The Houses of Nova Scotia

Although nature has given abundantly of her gifts to Nova Scotia, it is undoubtedly true that the variety and grace of the old buildings here contribute greatly to the charm of the province. It is steeped in history, and the pride of Nova Scotians in their achievements is evidenced in the care with which they preserve their buildings.

Wood is the most common material, and the wooden dwellings vary from the simplicity of Quaker-style frame houses, with no basement and exposed beam construction, to imposing Victorian dwellings, elaborated with fanciful gingerbread trim and elegant entranceways. Many houses are topped with a 'widow's walk', testament to the power of the sea and the marine heritage of so much of this province.

Shown here, a colourful doorway in Lunenburg and, opposite, a house in LaHave.

Church spires are reflected in the peaceful waters of Mahone Bay.

Boats tug at their lines at Blue Rocks.

Lunenburg

Opposite: Lunenburg is almost synonymous with fishing and fast schooners. Built on a peninsula with harbours front and back, the town is one of Canada's most important fishing areas. Founded by farmers who soon turned to the sea as the route to trade with Halifax, it has remained a primarily sea-oriented community. Most famous for its classic schooners, notably the *Bluenose*, today it still survives on fishing, fish processing, supplying equipment for vessels, and, of course, shipbuilding.

In the mid-1880s the first Lunenburg 'packet' was built — fast boats that could quickly negotiate the coastline to Halifax. The height of ship-building here was the small schooners — built to withstand the journey to the Grand Banks off Newfoundland, and to do it quickly, these fast and hardy boats became famous in fisheries up and down the Atlantic coast.

The Lunenburg Academy is a fine example of the imposing architecture of a former era.

Emerald islands lie off the Lunenburg coast.

The soil of Lunenburg County is rich and fertile, producing good crops for a local market.

Clark's Harbour, Cape Sable Island

Cape Sable Island is the southernmost point of Nova Scotia. It is dependent on fishing, boatbuilding and fish factories. The Cape Sable boat, first built here in 1907, is still the industry standard for small boats that must withstand the rigors of the North Atlantic.

Fishing in Nova Scotia

It is likely that fish brought the first European people to Nova Scotia, and the fishing industry has been integral to the life of the province ever since. Nova Scotians are proud of their marine heritage and a maritime flavour permeates even the most cosmopolitan centres. Of course, no part of Nova Scotia is far from the sea, and the entire shoreline is indented with coves and bays which have naturally become fishing ports.

Opposite: The tuna fleet up on stays at Wedgewood.

Yarmouth

The shipping tradition is very strong at Yarmouth. When sailing ships ruled the waves, Yarmouth had the third-largest merchant navy in the world, and boasted the world's highest per capita ship tonnage. Historically it has close ties with the United States — early settlers were Puritans from the U.S. and in 1785 many Loyalists arrived. These ties are maintained today and a ferry service operates from Yarmouth to Bar Harbour, Maine.

Today Yarmouth is the centre of fishing, dairying and agriculture as well as being an important fishing port. It preserves its history in many lovely museums, such as, the Firefighters Museum (Canada's only provincial firefighters museum) and the Yarmouth County Historical Society Museum, which has some award-winning displays. The area around here is especially scenic — Leif Erickson Picnic Park, named in honour of the Norseman who is thought to have journeyed to this area some 1000 years ago, overlooks a fabulous coastline.

Opposite: Marshlands at Surette Island.

Tiverton, Long Island

Geologists tell us that Long Island and Brier Island were once joined to the mainland. The rocky soil on the islands is exactly the same composition as that on the mainland. Now they are separated by Grand Passage and Petite Passage, and a year-round ferry service takes travellers to Tiverton, an important fishing port. From here it is possible to hire the services of a fisherman and boat to experience the thrill of a day of deep-sea fishing for cod, haddock or halibut, or to enjoy the superb scenery.

Opposite: Atlantic lobster is famous the world over and lobster pots are a common sight in Nova Scotia. On this dock at Tiverton they are being mended.

Churches

The many churches of Nova Scotia tell a story of hard work and faith, and each church has its own fascinating history.

St. Mary's Church at Church Point is the biggest wooden church in North America. Its steeple rises a full 55.5 m. (185 ft.), and requires 36 tonnes (40 tons) of ballast to hold it steady in the fierce offshore winds. The church at St. Bernard was an epic work which took 32 years for a population of 350 to complete; this huge stone church seats 1000. The Loyalist Church of St. Edward, built in 1788, is in Norman style, with hand-made hinges and nails. There are many more churches, each one a testament to the strength of faith of those early settlers. Opposite is St. Peter's Anglican Church, Murphy Cove.

Shed at Halfway River, a farming district north of Minas Basin.

Fort Anne

Nova Scotia was at the forefront of European settlement of Canada, and its history incorporates the struggle between France and England for control of the new colonies. Fort Anne National Historic Park was originally the site of an early Acadian settlement. Four forts have occupied this site, starting in 1635 when d'Aulnay de Charnisay established a French headquarters here. A small portion of these old walls is still visible. Since then French and English have battled over and taken this site no fewer than seven times, until 1854, when the garrison was dispersed. Fort Anne is now an historic park (Canada's first national historic park, established in 1917) with an historic library and a museum containing restored garrison rooms and an original Acadian room relocated from a homestead.

The Annapolis Valley

There are many agricultural areas in Nova Scotia but the Annapolis Valley is special. This rich valley, 160 km. (100 m.) long and 8-24 km (5 to 15 m.) wide, is sheltered from the winds and fog of the Atlantic by the North and South Mountains. The Annapolis River has been dyked for 32 km (20 m.) from its mouth, and this reclaimed land, which once flooded yearly, is a fertile alluvial composition which makes an excellent base for agricultural use. The most famous product of this region — in fact, famed world-wide — are the apples from the Annapolis Valley.

The Bay of Fundy

The land around the Bay of Fundy is well cultivated, as this aerial shows, and its coastline is ringed with small charming villages. When Champlain first saw the Bay of Fundy he wrote that it was "one of the most beautiful ports . . . seen on these coasts." Few people today would argue with that assessment.

The Bay of Fundy has the highest tides in the world. They range from 3.7 m (12 ft.) at Yarmouth, to 16.6 m. (54 ft.) at Burntcoat Head in Minas Basin. The Annapolis Royal Tidal Power Project, on the Annapolis Royal Causeway, is the first in North America to harness the tides for hydroelectric power.

Opposite: The Evangeline Church at Grand Pré is named after Longfellow's Acadian heroine, Evangeline.

Acadia and the Acadians

The struggle between France and England for control of the new colonies in North America is an integral part of the history of Canada, but nowhere is that struggle more poignant than in the story of the Acadians. When Nova Scotia, or Acadia as it was then known, was ceded to Britain in the Treaty of Utrecht, 1713, it signified the end of a way of life for the group of French settlers known as Acadians, whose roots in the area around Port Royal went back to 1605. They elected not to pledge an oath of allegiance to the English king, although they were assured freedom of worship and continuation of their way of life. They were expelled from the region; some moving west in Canada, some travelling south to Louisiana, there to form the basis of the Cajun tradition, centred around New Orleans, and some going to the United States and later returning.

The Acadian tradition is still strong in Nova Scotia, and along the French Shore — between Digby and Yarmouth — festivals and folklore ensure that this cultural stream will continue to survive.

Opposite: The traditional costume of an Acadian woman, at Nicolas Denys Museum in St. Peter's.

Northumberland Shore

The Northumberland shore has some of the finest beaches in Nova Scotia, and boasts the warmest salt water north of the Carolinas. The place names along this coast tell of a strong native Indian and Scottish heritage, and Antigonish is a centre for celebration of the Scottish tradition. Indian names like Tidnish — "a paddle", Shinimicas — "shining water", Malagash — "place of games" and Tatamagouche — "meeting place of the waters" are borrowed from the language of Nova Scotia's first people. New Annan, Balmoral Hills, Glengarry, New Glasgow and Arisaig are imported from Scotland — a touch of the familiar to those first settlers.

Interestingly, Pictou — settled primarily by passengers on the *Hector*, which sailed from Scotland in 1773 — got its name from the Indian 'Pictook' in 1790. Before that, the village was called Coleraine, New Paisley, Alexandria, Donegal, Southampton and Walmsley, in succession.

The Highland Games, held at Antigonish in mid-July include Scottish dancing, hammer-throws, caber tosses and ox-pulling events. These annual games have been held for over 120 years.

48

The beautiful slopes of the Clyburn Valley are beginning to show their fall colours.

The hills near Mabou, which is a centre for farming, dairying and sheep raising.

Cabot Trail

This route is rightfully considered to be one of the most scenic drives in North America. At every turn new vistas of sea, mountain and sky open up, and the road takes breathtaking turns, rising high into the craggy mountains and then dipping into the valleys below.

The route is named in honour of John Cabot, who first planted the flag of England here on Cape Breton soil in 1497. It is 296 km (184 m.) long, forming a loop which begins at Baddeck and continues around the northeastern coastline of Cape Breton, skirting the Cape Breton Highlands National Park, and ending again at the Bras d'Or Lake.

The beautiful Beulach Bann Falls.

An old dory hull bleaches in the sun at Aspy Bay.

The Keltic Lodge, near Ingonish Beach.

Ingonish Ferry, situated on the Cabot Trail.

Bras d'Or Lake

Bras d'Or Lake almost bisects Cape Breton Island, and is not really a lake at all, but an inland sea totalling 1005 km2 (450 sq. mi.). It is mildly salty, almost fog-free and has very little tide change, as the entrance to the lake is so narrow. Literally translated, the name means "arm of gold".

At St. Peter's, where a narrow strip of land separates Bras d'Or Lake from the Atlantic, a canal has been built. This allows boats to enter Bras d'Or Lake from St. Peter's Bay. Begun in 1854, the canal was completed in 1917.

Opposite: St. Patrick's Channel, near Baddeck on Bras d'Or Lake.

Fall in Nova Scotia is a time when the hills turn glorious shades of red, yellow, green and gold — a time to revel in the last warm days of summer before the cold winds whip in off the stormy Atlantic.

Maple trees are common here, and they not only play a part in this fall display, they are the basis of a thriving industry. In the Grande Anse Valley on Cape Breton, there are groves of huge maple trees over three hundred years old, and at Mapleton the maple products industry produces many thousands of kilograms (pounds) yearly from the trees in the Cobequid range.

Baddeck

Baddeck is situated on Bras d'Or Lake and marks the beginning and end of the Cabot Trail. The village has a population of less than 1000, swelled in the summer by an influx of people who own vacation homes in the area.

Baddeck has become a centre for yachting; it is in a central location for cruising the friendly waters of Bras d'Or and there are good trout fishing waters nearby.

The name derives from the Micmac 'Abadak' meaning place with an island near — which most probably refers to Kidston's Island in Baddeck Harbour.

Opposite: Alexander Graham Bell National Historic Park at Baddeck.

Alexander Graham Bell Museum

Born in Scotland, and an American citizen, Alexander Graham Bell discovered the beauty of the area around Baddeck in 1885. Here he made his summer home, carried out many experiments and was eventually buried. Best known for his invention of the telephone, Alexander Graham Bell was a man of diverse talents. Throughout his life he continued to experiment in different fields. In 1909 he launched his *Silver Dart* on Bras d'Or Lake, marking the first man-powered flight in the British Commonwealth. He was also a humanitarian who is well known for his work with Helen Keller.

Opposite: The Alexander Graham Bell National Historic Park and Museum opened in 1956 to commemorate Bell's achievements. He and his wife were buried at their home, Beinn Breagh, near Baddeck, on a cliff overlooking the land they loved.

Coal has been mined for three centuries in Cape Breton. In 1673, seams of coal were visible in the cliffs around Bras d'Or, and by 1720 there was organized mining at Cow Bay (now called Port Morien). This was the first such operation in North America; coal was mined for those working on the construction of Fortress Louisbourg. By 1724 coal was being exported to Boston.

Until 1950 coal played a major role in the economy of Nova Scotia. While it is still being mined here, availability of other forms of energy have affected the industry. Cities such as Sydney are based on coal; developed because of the rich coal beds, it is still its major economic support. Sydney also has one of North America's largest steel plants.

Glace Bay and Springhill also have a coal-based economy. The Miner's Museum at Springhill chronicles the early days of coalmining, with a tour underground of a coal shaft.

Opposite: A blast furnace at Sydney.

Fortress Louisbourg

Fortress Louisbourg was begun in 1713, took 20 years to complete, and was destroyed by 1760. It was built to protect the interests of King Louis XV of France in the new world, and when it fell to the British, its walls torn down and its people exiled, it marked the end of an era.

While it stood, Fortress Louisbourg was the centre of a rich and complex life. Within its walls, 3 m. thick and 9 m. high (10 ft. and 30 ft.) was a unique blend of the opulence of 18th Century France and the rough and ready opportunities of the New World. The houses of the wealthy and powerful stood next to the simple dwellings of the workers. Established as the military capital of a colony, it was a place of war and an example to all of the strength and magnificence of the French government it represented.

After its fall, Fortress Louisbourg was deserted, and new centres of commerce and government were started elsewhere, creating a rarity — a once powerful fortress town which has not been obliterated by a modern city. Today we can enjoy Fortress Louisbourg, a large portion faithfully reconstructed and restored to its original state, complete with soldiers, servants and households. At one time Fortress Louisbourg was the greatest fort in North America. A visitor today can relive that busy life, even to having a meal in an authentic tavern — the simple food of the times, served on a pewter plate and eaten with a dagger!

Opposite: The Governor's dining room at Louisbourg.

Photo Credits
P. 10: J. A. Kraulis; p. 11: Ted Czolowski; p. 12, 13, 14: J. A. Kraulis; p. 15: Cosmo Condina; p. 16, 17, 19: J. A. Kraulis; p. 19: John Burridge, Photo/Graphics; p. 20: J. A. Kraulis; p. 21: Ted Czolowski; p. 22, 23: Jurgen Vogt, Photo/Graphics; p. 24: Cosmo Condina; p. 25, 26, 27: Jurgen Vogt, Photo/Graphics; p. 28, 29, 30, 31: J. A. Kraulis; p. 33: Fraser Clark; p. 34, 35, 36, 37: J. A. Kraulis; p. 38: Jurgen Vogt, Photo/Graphics; p. 39, 41: Cosmo Condina; p. 42: Gunter Marx, Photo/Graphics; p. 43, 44: J. A. Kraulis; p. 45: Wayne Lynch; p. 47: Warren Gordon; p. 48: Andrius Valadka; p. 49: Sherman Hines; p. 50, 51, 53, 54: Warren Gordon; p. 55: Fraser Clark; p. 56, 57: Warren Gordon; p. 59, 60, 61: John Burridge, Photo/Graphics; p. 62: J. A. Kraulis; p. 63, 65: John Burridge, Photo/Graphics; p. 66, 67: Warren Gordon; p. 69: John Burridge, Photo/Graphics; p. 70, 71: Warren Gordon; p. 72: John Burridge, Photo/Graphics.